A DAY IN THE LIFE OF A
KNIGHT

Andrea Hopkins

Illustrated by Inklink, Firenze

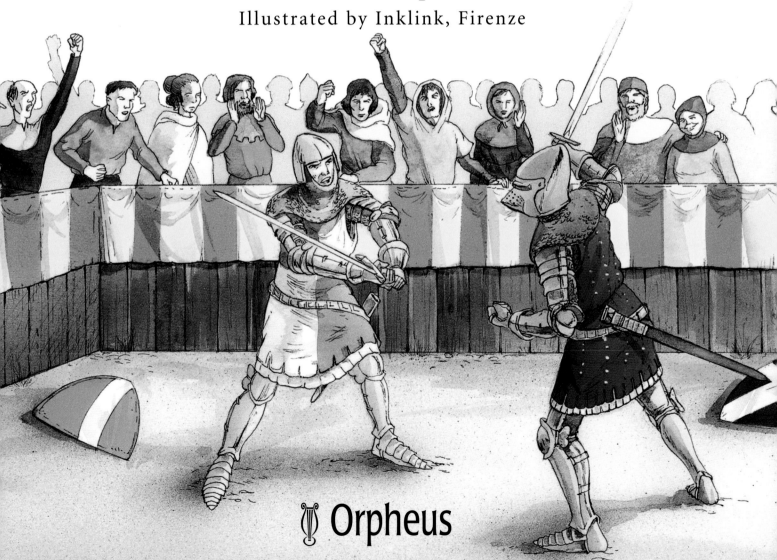

Orpheus

First published in 2006 by Orpheus
Books Ltd., 6 Church Green, Witney,
Oxfordshire, OX28 4AW.
Copyright © 2006 Orpheus Books Ltd.

Created and produced by Emma Godfrey,
Emma Helbrough, Rachel Coombs,
Nicholas Harris and Sarah Hartley,
Orpheus Books Ltd.

ISBN 1 905473 02 8

A CIP record for this book is available from
the British Library.

Printed and bound in Malaysia.

CONTENTS

ABOUT THIS BOOK

In this fascinating book you will follow a very busy day in the life of a knight in medieval Europe. Along the way, you will learn all about what life was like for a knight, from his courtly duties to the food he ate and the games he played.

HUNTING

The Baron and his knights have gone hunting on horseback. Guy follows on foot. Not far from the castle he meets a group of young people out hawking. Among them is Lady Felice. Guy stops to speak to her and admires her falcon, a merlin. Felice shows him how the bird is trained to fly at her command, catch small birds in the air and return to her.

Suddenly there is a sound of galloping hooves and baying hounds. The hunt almost bursts upon them, hot in pursuit of a roebuck deer. If they catch the deer, it will be eaten for dinner in a few days.

Knight's Knowledge
As well as deer, which other animals would knights have hunted?
a) Wild boars
b) Wolves
c) Bears

16   17

This is Sir Guy de Frinton. He is the main character in this story.

Look out for a flap to lift on almost every double page.

TELLING THE TIME

There is a clock in the corner of each page, so you can check what time it is in the story, but in truth most people didn't use mechanical clocks like this one to tell the time. In medieval Europe mechanical clocks were only found on cathedral clock towers. Sundials were more commonly used.

Sundials work using the position of the sun. The hours are marked around the edge of a sundial and in the middle there is a pointer called a style. As the sun moves across the sky, it causes the style's shadow to move too. You can tell the time by seeing what hour the shadow points to.

These illustrations show a sundial at three different times of the day.

MEDIEVAL EUROPE

In Europe the period from about AD500 to 1500 is known as the Middle Ages, or the medieval period. This story is set towards the end of that era in the 15th century.

Life was very organized in medieval Europe. There were four levels of society. At the top was the king, who owned all the land, made laws and led armies.

Below the king were the nobles. He gave them land in return for their promise to fight for him whenever needed. Knights were the next level of society. They worked for nobles, training and fighting in battles with them for the king.

At the bottom of society were the peasants. They farmed the land belonging to the nobles and knights.

In medieval Europe, townsfolk had to apply for permission from the king to hold a market in the town square each week.

5

ON THE ROAD

Sir Guy de Frinton and his squire, William de Lacy, are hungry. It is eight o'clock in the morning when they arrive at the market town of Barton, but they have been on the road since five. They are on their way to Belmont Castle to take part in a tournament and have stopped at an inn to order a good breakfast. While it is being prepared, they will do some shopping. It is market day and the streets are busy with farmers, traders and town craftsmen.

Sir Guy hands William a purse full of money and tells him to buy ale, cheese, bread, beeswax, salt, oil and other supplies.

As Sir Guy waits for William, he listens to a herald announcing the tournament. The townsfolk love a good tournament. They are always exciting to watch and provide a chance to make money!

Fact or fiction?
Knights rescued damsels in distress.

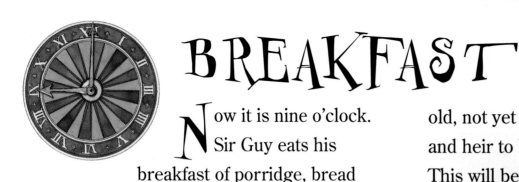

BREAKFAST

Now it is nine o'clock. Sir Guy eats his breakfast of porridge, bread and cold meat, washed down with ale. The landlord knows all the gossip, so Guy asks him about the tournament—who is taking part, who will be watching—as well as about the castle and its owner. In return, he tells the landlord about himself. He is 24 years old, not yet married, and an only son and heir to his father's two estates. This will be his ninth tournament.

Fact or fiction?

Knights went on quests in search of the holy grail.

Guy hasn't won a tournament yet, but he has worked hard and is eager to do well. The landlord thinks he looks like a strong, determined young man. Guy is quietly confident. Today may be his day!

Meanwhile, in the stable, William is looking after the horses. They have three: Guy's huge, powerful warhorse, Gringolet; William's riding horse, Tirant, and their packhorse, Dobbin. Dobbin carries all their luggage, armour and equipment, strapped to a wooden frame on his back. Gringolet is a heavy horse, specially bred to be strong enough to carry a knight in full armour.

THE CASTLE

At about ten o'clock, Sir Guy and William arrive at Belmont Castle, home of Baron Richard Fitzroy. Guy's mother is related to the Baron's wife, Lady Margery Fitzroy, so Guy will stay in the castle, instead of in a tent outside with the other competitors. Baron Fitzroy is wealthy and powerful. His castle has all the latest defences: a new "curtain" wall, a moat and a large gatehouse with a portcullis. Guy and William are very impressed.

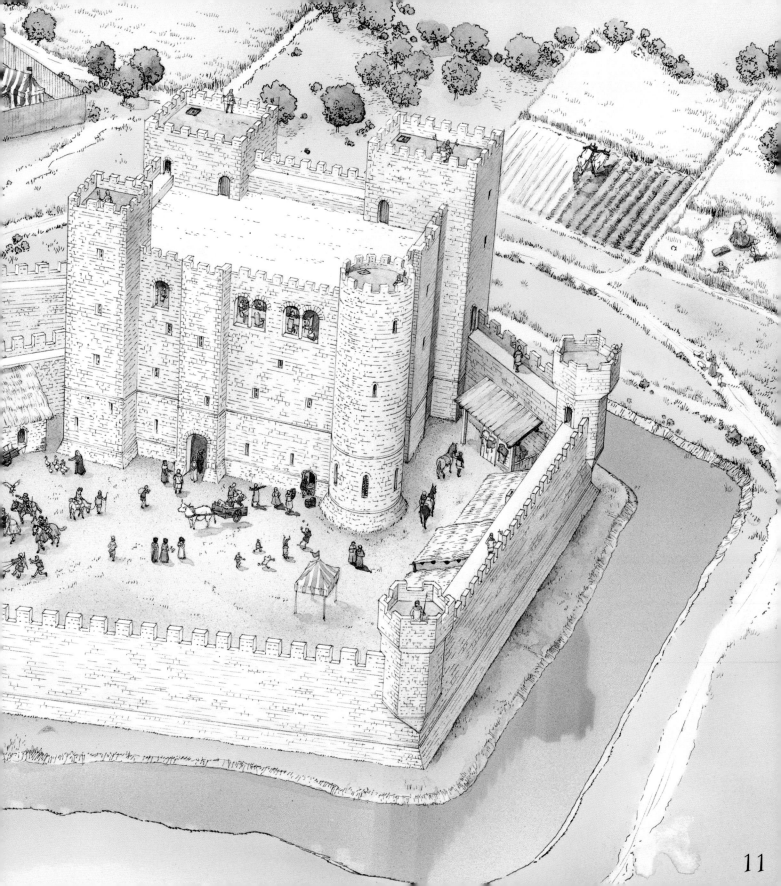

CHIVALRY

Guy goes to the castle's chapel to pray for strength and good luck in the tournament. There he meets Lady Felice, the Baron's youngest daughter. She is 18 and astonishingly beautiful, or so Guy thinks. As a knight, he must be courteous to ladies, so he goes down on one knee to kiss her hand, as if she were the queen.

Felice should have been married this year, but her fiancé died unexpectedly. She had never met him; her parents arranged the marriage when she was just a child. Felice reads lots of romance stories, and would rather marry for love. She likes Guy; he is very handsome and has excellent manners.

Guy has been training to be a knight since he was 10 years old. He is very fit: he can ride and fight in full armour, he can hit a small target with a lance at full gallop, and he can leap from the ground into Gringolet's saddle. William hopes to become a knight himself in a few years' time. They both take great pride in keeping Guy's armour and weapons in top condition.

While Guy is at the chapel, William goes to the forge to mend a tear in Guy's chain-mail shirt. Guy inherited it from his grandfather. New ones cost a whole year's income. It could save his life in battle, so any tears or rusty spots are carefully mended.

Fact or fiction?
Knights fought dragons.

ENTERTAINMENT

Guy wanders around the castle grounds to see what is going on. He stops to watch some men having an archery contest. The archers use their longbows to shoot at raised targets called butts, which are made of straw. The targets are gradually moved further

and further away. A good archer can hit the target from 200 metres away and in this game there is a clear winner.

Guy enjoys watching a good game of archery, but like all knights he does not play the sport himself. The bow is considered an unchivalrous weapon because it is used to kill from a distance, so knights always choose close combat weapons instead.

Further on, Guy sees people playing a game called "Kayles". This is a bit like ten-pin bowling, except you throw a club at the pins instead of bowling a ball, and there are nine pins not ten.

Another favourite with the crowd is a troupe of minstrels. They can do many things to entertain people: dance, sing, play instruments, tell stories,

juggle, walk on stilts, balance things on their heads, twist their bodies into strange shapes, and do acrobatics. The acrobats are called tumblers.

Knight's Knowledge

Which of these games was played in medieval times?

a) Football
b) Chess
c) Hockey

15

HUNTING

The Baron and his knights have gone hunting on horseback. Guy follows on foot. Not far from the castle he meets a group of young people out hawking. Among them is Lady Felice. Guy stops to speak to her and admires her falcon, a merlin. Felice shows him how the bird is trained to fly at her command, catch small birds in the air and return to her.

Suddenly there is a sound of galloping hooves and baying hounds. The hunt almost bursts upon them, hot in pursuit of a roebuck deer. If they catch the deer, it will be eaten for dinner in a few days.

Knight's Knowledge

As well as deer, which other animals would knights have hunted?

a) Wild boars
b) Wolves
c) Bears

ARMING

It is now two o'clock. The tournament will begin in an hour, so Guy has to begin getting ready. Each layer of armour has to be buckled into place, so William helps him. First, Guy puts on a padded undercoat, which stops the armour rubbing uncomfortably against his skin.

Next, he puts on a long-sleeved tunic of chain mail called a hauberk. Over this he wears a coat-of-plates, which is another padded tunic reinforced with metal plates. This will protect him from stab wounds. William now buckles Guy's plate armour on to his legs and arms.

His hands are protected by padded metal gloves called gauntlets, and over his head and shoulders he wears an aventail, a sort of chain-mail hood. His helmet goes on top of this. Guy is now wearing half his own body weight in armour.

Over the armour, Guy wears a surcoat in his personal colour, red. William slings his shield over one shoulder and hands Guy his lance. The shield is painted with Guy's personal emblem, known as a coat of arms. Now when his face is hidden behind the helmet, the people watching will know who he is.

Fully armed, Guy feels a rush of excitement. He is now ready for the tournament to begin. While Guy says a final prayer, William goes to the stables to saddle up Gringolet.

PARADING

Before the tournament commences, the knights parade around the barrier while the crowds cheer them on. Some people make bets on who will win.

Felice recognizes Guy and beckons him over. She gives him a token—a silk scarf. This means Guy is fighting for her; he is her knight. It also means she really likes him, which makes him very happy.

The tournament will begin with jousting. Two knights charge at one another on either side of the barrier and try to knock each other off their horses.

he smashes his lance against his opponent's shield. If there is no clear winner, the heralds decide who has won.

In the final round, the jousting is followed by sword fighting on foot. The two competitors fight until only one man is left standing.

JOUSTING

Knowing that Felice is watching him makes Guy feel even braver. No-one can beat him, and he reaches the final round. His opponent is Sir Huon of Bordeaux, an older and more experienced knight.

22

The first two encounters are even; each knight breaks a lance. At the third encounter, Guy's lance shatters, but he almost loses his seat, so the heralds judge it to be a tie. The contest will continue on foot, and this time he MUST win. Guy reaches for his sword.

23

SWORD FIGHT

It is now after five o'clock on a hot July afternoon. The knights have been competing in their heavy armour for more than two hours, but the thought of winning the tournament gives them new energy.

For a few minutes the roar of the crowd is almost drowned out by the clang of swords against armour. Both knights are so well armed that neither of them is seriously wounded, although they are both tired and aching.

Guy feels boiling hot beneath all his armour and padding. He can't wipe the sweat from his eyes with his visor down, so he raises it.

Now he can see properly, although his face is unprotected. He sees that Sir Huon is exhausted by the heat—his face is dark red and he is gasping for breath. At last, Guy forces him to his knees, and he cannot get up. Sir Huon surrenders. Guy has won!

Fact or fiction?

There are still knights around today.

VICTORY!

The crowd cheers for Guy—especially the people who bet on him! As Guy raises his sword to salute the crowd, he can feel his arms ache. His chain mail has protected him from deep stab wounds, but not from bruises. He knows that when William takes his armour off, he will be black and blue all over. But right now he just doesn't care!

Lady Margery allows her daughter Felice to present Guy with his prize. It is a jewelled pin that he can use to fasten his cloak. To Guy, the fame and reputation he will gain from winning are much more valuable than any jewel.

Knight's Knowledge

When knights took castles by siege, what did they often catapult over the castle walls?

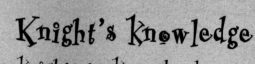

a) Dead animals
b) Buckets of water
c) Lead weights

Many rich and powerful lords were watching the tournament, and one of them will certainly offer him a job.

But the look in Felice's eyes when she puts the jewel in his hand is the best thing of all. Felice is very proud that her knight won the tournament, and very relieved that he is not injured. Tournaments are safer than they used to be, but knights are still sometimes killed.

Feeling both exhausted and elated, Guy returns to the castle for a well-earned rest. He knows he must make a speedy recovery because the Baron is planning a great feast in his honour for that evening. For Guy this will mean plenty of opportunites to talk to Felice...

FEASTING

Guy has never seen such a lavish feast as the one that takes place in Baron Fitzroy's Great Hall that evening. The Baron congratulates Guy on winning and offers him a place in his household. Guy rushes over to Felice and tells her the good news. As one of her father's knights, they will be able to see each other every day. It has been a *very* good day!

Knight's Knowledge

Roughly how many courses were eaten during a feast?

a) Three
b) Ten
c) Twenty

GLOSSARY

Here you can check the meaning of some of the words in this book.

Falcon

archery	—	A sport involving shooting with bows and arrows at a target.
baron	—	A land-holding nobleman.
beeswax	—	A type of wax produced by bees, which is used to make ointments and polishes.
chain mail	—	A piece of clothing or fabric made from thousands of tiny metal rings linked together by hand.
chivalry	—	The idea of how knights should behave.
coat of arms	—	A knight's personal emblem, originally sewn on to his coat.
forge	—	A place where metal is heated and hammered into shape.
gatehouse	—	The entrance to a castle.
hawking	—	Hunting using birds of prey such as hawks and falcons.
herald	—	A messenger who oversaw tournaments.
inn	—	A small hotel or pub providing food and lodging.
jousting	—	A game in which two knights on horseback try to knock one another off their horse using a weapon called a lance.

longbow	—	A large bow which was widely used in medieval times.
minstrel	—	A musician, singer and poet.
moat	—	A wide ditch, filled with water, surrounding a castle.
portcullis	—	A metal gate at the entrance to a castle, which could be lowered to keep attackers out.
squire	—	A young nobleman who looked after a knight.
tournament	—	A sporting event for knights in which they competed for a prize.
visor	—	A piece of armour attached to a helmet that covers and protects the face.

The layout of a castle

1. Keep
2. Curtain wall
3. Gatehouse
4. Portcullis
5. Moat

INDEX